NEEDLEPOINT:
Design Your Own

Geranium and ribbon pillow *worked by Mrs. Irving Rubicoff*

NEEDLEPOINT:
Design Your Own

Muriel Baker
Barbara Eyre
Margaret Wall
Charlotte Westerfield

Charles Scribner's Sons / New York

Library of Congress Cataloging in Publication Data
Main entry under title:

Needlepoint: design your own.

Bibliography: p.
1. Canvas embroidery.   I. Baker, Muriel L.
TT778.C3N44   746.4′4   73–19291
ISBN 0-684-14867-6

1 3 5 7 9 11 13 15 17 19 M/P 20 18 16 14 12 10 8 6 4 2

Printed in the United States of America

Library of Congress Cataloging in Publication Data

Acknowledgements

How do you say thank you to all those who have helped in the writing of this book? So many contributed in so many ways. To all those we give our heartfelt thanks. Special thanks are due Ryan Kuhn, whose idea it was; Ginger Tayntor, for her help in the chapter on mounting; Maura Beaucar and Susan Nuss for much help with the drawings; Harold Pratt, our photographer, for his skill and patience; Edith Panaro, who typed our manuscript; and last but not least three, husbands and one sister, Jim Eyre, Wayne Wall, John Westerfield and Marion Lewis who stood steadfastly by, always ready with an apt suggestion or different angle. Our sincere appreciation also to our Editor, Elinor Parker—one author can be a trial—but four!

Muriel Baker
Barbara Eyre
Margaret Wall
Charlotte Westerfield

Owls on branch *worked by Mrs. Francis Parsons*

Contents

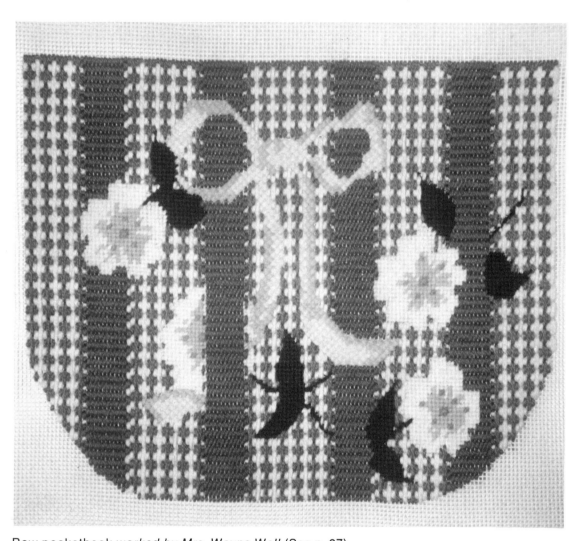

Bow pocketbook *worked by Mrs. Wayne Wall* (See p. 37)

Introduction

Can you design your own needlepoint? . . . . YES!!!

Now that more and more people are doing needlepoint, and doing it well, more and more people are wishing they could design their own. Well, with the help of this book, you will be able to do just that.

You don't have to be a Picasso or a Matisse, or to have had formal art training to turn your own ideas into needlepoint. You do have to have patience, a feeling for color, some drawing or tracing ability, a chance to practice . . . and patience. Anyone who has decorated a room, put together an interesting wardrobe, or planned a garden has the talents to design needlepoint. But like a garden, a good design takes time to grow. We make design decisions every day without realizing it. So what seems to be needed is a way to organize our thoughts with some practical know-how, so that they can be translated into personal needle-point design.

There is no reason to do pillow after pillow, although, as a starting project, a pillow is a simple one. But why not start some design that's unusual and more fun? Try a game table top, a mirror frame worked in many different stitches, a tennis racket cover, or an address book for that man who has everything, featuring his hobbies, foibles, occupation, even his pre-occupa-tion, or simply his monogram.

There are so many interesting ways needlepoint can be used, unlimited opportunities for artistic expression, so many glorious colors and textured yarns available on the market, and so many exciting designs all around us from which to draw, that it's a shame many qualified persons are timid about starting their own designs. Have confidence!

Actually we were a bit timid, too, when we started our needlepoint business. But we were also bored with the designs that were on the market and horrified at some of the prices. With patience and practice we turned our timid beginning into a thriving business with a retail shop in Farmington, Connecticut, carrying our exclusive designs and a growing wholesale business.

Here, then, are the tools and knowledge you will need.

NEEDLEPOINT:
Design Your Own

Materials for Design

MATERIALS NEEDED

Before beginning to design, assemble the materials needed and set up a work area, which does not need to be a permanent spot, but one where things can be left undisturbed for a while. First acquire

> 1 Large Plywood Board
> Roll of white shelf paper
> Masking tape
> Thumb tacks

The board can be placed on any convenient table. It must have a surface that will take tacks. A good size is 24 x 48 inches, but it can be smaller unless a large project is planned. A bread board will do in some cases. The board should be covered by taping the shelf paper onto it to make the design easier to see when it is traced onto the canvas.

> Black waterproof India ink
> Speedball pen point
> Holder and Point #A-5 is a good size
> Good quality water color brushes

The two most popular size brushes are #14 and #16; these will hold a nice point and can be used for both large and small areas. A one-inch brush is good if there are large areas to paint as in the background.

Drawing pads
Pencils
Erasers
Ruler
Tracing paper

Tracing paper comes in various sized pads. For a large project a roll of tracing paper can be bought at any art supply store as can all of the items on above list.

Aluminum coffee cake tins
Mason jars

The tins make a good palette, the Mason jars will hold water, pencils and brushes. A child's lunch box or a fishing tackle box make good paint tube containers. All these materials are easily put away when not in use. (See Figure 1)

Two types of paint—oils and acrylics—are used for painting needlepoint. Acrylics are preferable as they dry very quickly and are mixed with water, and the brushes are cleaned with water. Oils take at least twenty-four hours to dry and the clean-up is

Figure 1

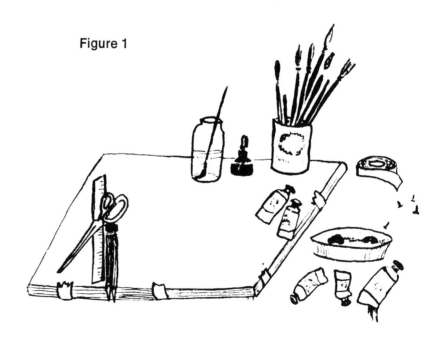

with turpentine. Whichever paint is chosen, it is essential that a good quality paint be used as it *must* be waterproof. It is essential that *all* materials used in designing needlepoint be waterproof, because after the piece has been stitched, it is washed and blocked. Any non-waterproof ink or paint will run onto the wool and nothing will ever get it out. Many colored, felt-tip markers are not waterproof, and while they are quick and easy to use they will be a nightmare in the long run. The basic colors needed are:

White	Black
Ultramarine	Cerulean blue
Hookers green	Permanent green light
Alizarin crimson	Cadmium red
Cadmium Yellow	Hansa yellow light
Yellow ochre	Raw sienna
Burnt sienna	Burnt umber

If oils are used, they are thinned with the following mixture:

⅓ Boiled linseed oil
⅓ Damar varnish
⅓ Turpentine

This can be mixed and stored in a jar and used in small quantities as needed.

CANVAS

There are many types of canvas, but the two kinds used most in this country are penelope canvas and mono-canvas. Penelope canvas has a double warp and a double weft and can be used in the same way as mono-canvas, or the threads may be separated to form a smaller mesh. Mono-canvas has a single warp and weft and, since it is the easiest and most preferable to work with, it is discussed fully. Mono-canvas comes in many sized meshes, as small as 40 holes to the inch (petit point) to rug canvas that could be 5 holes to the inch. (gros point) The sizes most generally used are 18, 16, 14, or 12. It is important when designing to keep the canvas size in mind. If intricate shading and lines are planned, you will want to use a small mesh canvas. Also, small pieces such as a coin purse, glasses case or man's

Penelope canvas (double strand) and Mono canvas (single strand)

belt call for small mesh canvas. (The smaller the mesh the larger the number.)

Number 18 mesh canvas takes one strand of crewel or Persian yarn to do diagonal stitches. Number 16, still a fine canvas, takes two strands of wood, therefore, shading can be more subtle. This shading should also be considered when the design is being planned. Number 14 mesh is most often used because it is fine enough to do detailed designs, yet large enough to be easily seen and quicker to work up than #18 or #16.

It would be foolish and frustrating, for instance, to put a small, delicate design on canvas with too large a mesh. Details are only as fine as the stitch size, no matter how fine it is painted.

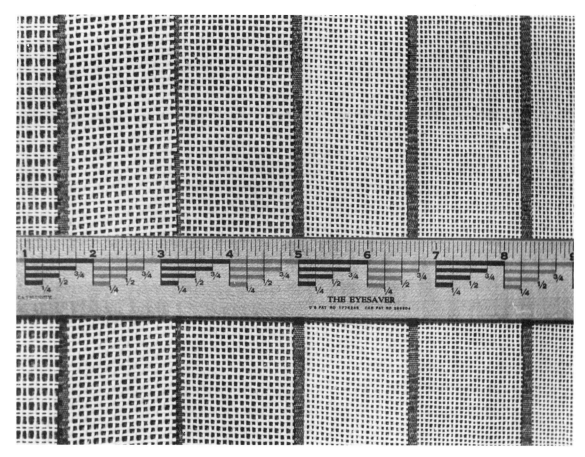

Different size meshes of canvas (left to right); #5, 10, 12, 14, 16, & 18.

On too large a mesh, much of the design would be lost. Conversely why waste time doing a design with large simple areas on fine canvas—especially as the larger, coarser texture of a #10 or #12 mesh might add interest to a simple design?

WOOL

It is not necessary to purchase the wool before the design is done, but it would be smart, somewhere along the line, to visit a friendly local needlepoint store and see what type of wool is available—how much it will cost, what colors it comes in and how many shades of each color.

The two most commonly used wools today are Persian wool, which comes 3-ply and is a flat wool with some sheen to it, and crewel wool which comes single ply, is round, and has no sheen. Both types of wool come in a glorious assortment of colors, from the traditional, subdued colors to the more vivid, contemporary colors, and both have three to four, even as many as six, shadings of each color.

Designs are all around, start looking, that might be half the fun!

There are 16 color plates after page 54.

Designing for Canvas

Design is difficult to define. Webster's dictionary, among many definitions, says, "a design is a plan or idea intended to be expressed in visible form," also that a design is "an arrangement of details." Both of these definitions relate to the designing of canvas embroidery. The work so commonly called "needlepoint" is really canvas embroidery or canvas work. Using the dictionary again, needlepoint is defined as "lace wrought wholly with a needle". Needlepoint, probably first done in ancient Egypt about the 4th century B.C., was referred to as canvas work or canvas embroidery until around the turn of the twentieth century, when it became known as needlepoint. The misnomer has remained.

When designing for needlepoint, as in all other designing, a few simple rules must be followed if the resulting work is to be pleasing. The eye expects and enjoys certain things. If the design fulfills these expectations, it is successful. If not, the eye does not care to linger and will quickly reject it. One of the first necessities of a good composition is to keep the eye from running out of the picture. (See Plate 1) In this design the eye follows the trailing strawberry vine, from its point of impact with the three strawberries to where it turns inward at the right edge. The butterfly also helps keep the eye from wandering.

The form and the shape of the space to be decorated is an important determining factor in any design. Use is another basic factor, as is how much or how little decoration should be placed on the allotted space. Some design decisions are, of course, a matter of personal taste and will vary. But if the few basic rules given here are followed, they will help insure a design that will not only catch the eye but will cause it to linger with pleasure. (See Plate 2) The first thing to greet your eye on this mirror frame is the color and the majesty of the spires of delphinium, then the humming birds, so skillfully drawn that they appear in motion. The sides and the bottom of the frame are well filled with design while the top is pleasantly open, like a garden on a summer day.

UNITY

Any design must form a perfect whole. Each component must be drawn and integrated to achieve Unity. Unity can be achieved by theme, by color, by line and often by a combination of these elements. (See Plate 3) In this piece the desired unity is achieved in all three ways. Unity in the piece illustrated in Plate 4 is achieved by the strength of the focal point and the subordination of all else in the design to it.

The Greeks in the 5th century B.C. formulated a mathematical science of art known as "dynamic symmetry." Following this principle we find a good way to visualize the proper placement of the center of interest. Divide the space to be filled into thirds, both horizontally and vertically. Near the intersections of these lines are the best places for the center of interest. (See Figure 2)

It is important that an idea, a color, or a striking line be DOMINANT in any design. In the quail design, it is the idea. (See Plate 5) The color is dominant in the stylized bouquet of strawberries. (See Plate 6) The line in the design of the saucy woodpecker is all important to the pleasing quality. Lines can be very important because they express so much in themselves. Some lines suggest quiet and repose, some grace and beauty, some energy, action and motion, and some strength on the next page.

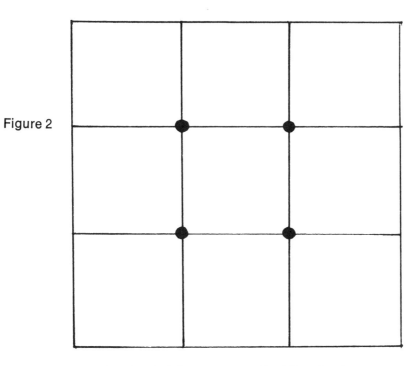

Figure 2

Woodpecker brick—strong vertical line dominant

Figure 3

Vertical lines suggest dignity, grandeur and strength and often have a formal effect on the eye. (See Figure 3)

Horizontal lines express calm, repose and restfulness. They have a tendency to quiet the eye. (See Figure 4)

Diagonal lines suggest a strength and action, often sharp, violent action. (See Figure 5)

Figure 4

Figure 5

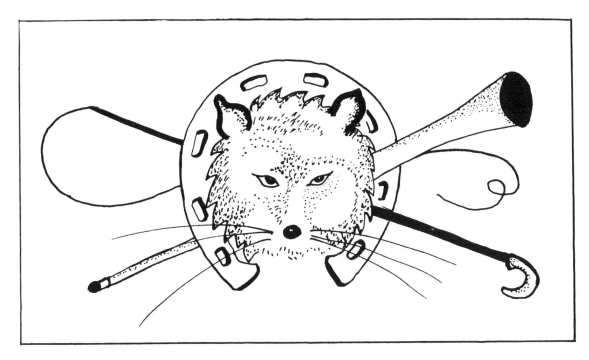

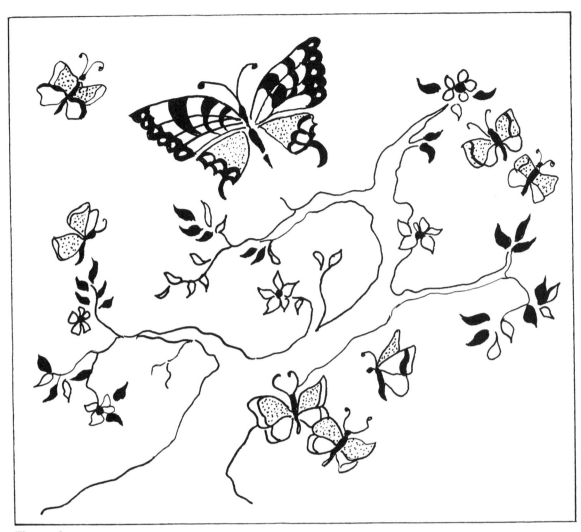

Figure 6

Curved lines are suggestive of grace, beauty, and gentle movement, as opposed to a diagonal line's impression of quick movement. (See Figure 6)

The S Curve, generally regarded as the most beautiful of all lines, is often called "the line of beauty." A composition based on this line is sure to please the eye. (See Figure 7)

Figure 7

Wrong

Figure 8

Right

PROPORTION
Every good design has good Proportion. The units must be proportioned to themselves and the design must be in proportion to the space to be filled. The open spaces of the design must also be considered. (See Plate 7) The most common mistake made is that the proportion of the design to the space to be filled is not correct. Too often it is too small, rarely is it too large. (See Figure 8)

CONTRAST
The eye soon becomes satiated with recurring or repeating design and demands a Contrast. This contrast can be achieved by color, content, line, or the introduction of the unexpected into the design. (See Figure 9)

RHYTHM
An old song that suggests, if you've got rhythm, why ask for anything more. And, indeed, Rhythm goes a long way toward making

Figure 9

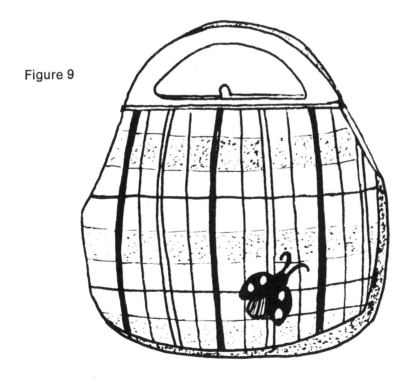

Mallard—grasses repeat the rhythmical lines of the bird

a pleasing design. Similar lines, shapes and colors within a design cause the eye to react favorably to the whole. It is carried along without effort through the units and voids.

BALANCE
And lastly, Balance occurs when opposing forces neutralize each other. Without balance the composition would be poor indeed. (See Figure 10) There are two kinds of balance
Symmetrical—if a line is drawn down the middle of the composition, the two halves would be of equal weight. Often they would be identical, or mirror, images.

Wrong

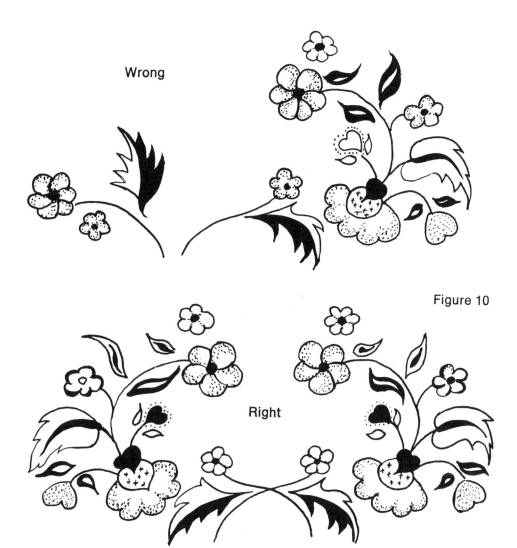

Figure 10

Right

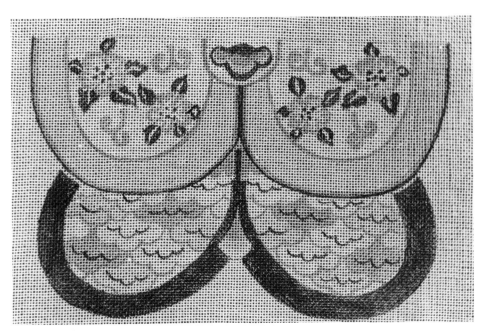

Butterfly wings are mirror image

Hummingbird and wisteria for assymetrical design

Asymmetrical design, where the two halves are of unequal weight. Good design must be achieved by the placement of shape or color. Asymmetrical balance is harder to achieve than symmetrical, but once accomplished it is generally more pleasing.

As lines help to convey certain thoughts in a design, so do shapes. For example, a **Circle** expresses continued movement and does a lot to keep the eye from wandering. Often the center of interest is within the circle.

The **Rectangle** is a quiet shape and suggest dignity and peace. When using this form it is good to have a single upright figure near the side, with small objects on the other side to achieve balance and interest.

Frog circle

Upright owl balances two small chickadees

Pyramid of Iris

The **Pyramid** or **Triangle** is the most used of all the basic shapes. It has great stability and strength, leads the eye to a climax, and is easy to follow. In most of the religious paintings of the 16th century the great masters used the triangle composition.

Figure 11

The **Cross** is a forceful form that creates harmony and unity. It draws strong attention to the place where the lines cross.

Radii give the feeling of both attraction and diffusion. They suggest joyous movement. Petals of flowers and branches of trees have this feeling of movement. The center of interest should be near the hub.

When designing, keep these simple rules in mind. They will help achieve good design. Soon, through experience, the rules will become second nature and can be used in a more flexible way. As they become more and more automatic, they become a part of your own personal expression in design.

Female mallard suggests joyous movement

Color

COLOR WHEEL

The treat in today's world of needlepoint is the vast selection of beautifully colored yarns. Most colors have from three to five values to choose from.

When in doubt about a color scheme, rely on the traditional color wheel.

If a few basic rules are followed, it should not be hard to put together an attractive color scheme. First, turn to the color wheel. (See Plate 8)

1. **Complementary colors** are two colors that are opposite each other on the color wheel, such as red and green. (See Plate 9)
2. **Analogous colors** are two colors that are next to each other on the wheel, such as green and blue-green. (See Plate 8)
3. **Split Complement**—use of two colors; one basic, the other is the color or colors on either side of the complement. For example, orange is opposite blue, the split complement of orange would be either blue violet or blue green. (See Plate 10 and Figures 12 and 13 on p. 26)
4. **Monochromatic scheme**—use of one color in different tints, shades and intensities. This is particularly effective when using different stitches and can produce sophisticated results. (See Plate 11 and Diagram 19, p. 52)

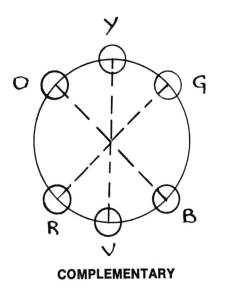

COMPLEMENTARY

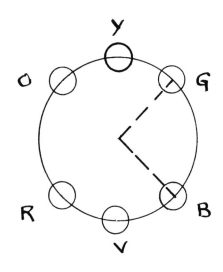

ANALAGOUS

Figure 12

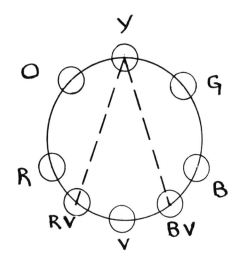

SPLIT COMPLEMENT

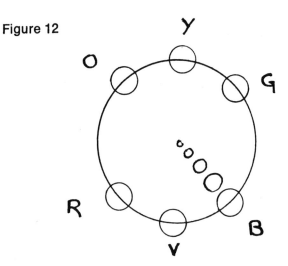

MONOCHROMATIC

COLOR TIPS

One word of caution. Be careful not to use too many colors. It is far more effective to use two or three colors, especially when beginning. (See Plate 12)

Another effective scheme is to use pale tones of bright colors, all the same values in an overall design, such as greens, pinks, yellows, purples. (See Plate 13)

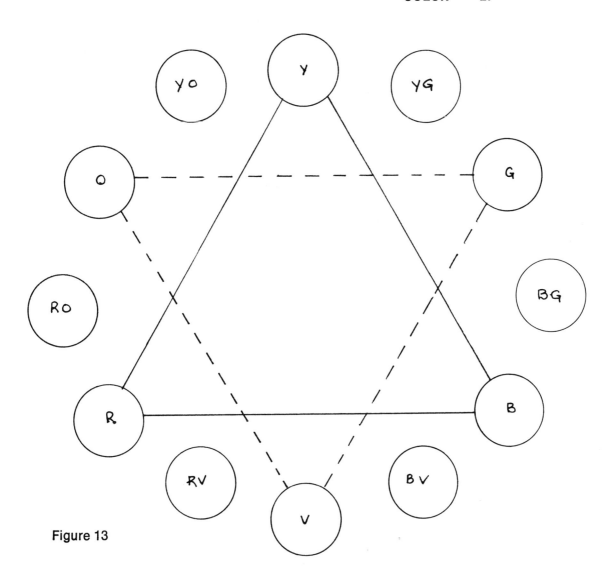

Figure 13

COLOR CHART

Y — Yellow
YG — Yellow
G — Green
BG — Blue Green
B — Blue
BV — Blue Violet

V — Violet
RV — Red Violet
R — Red
RO — Red Orange
O — Orange
YO — Yellow Orange

A word about background color. It is very important to decide on the background color to be used before painting in the colors of the design.

If there is a dark background, the values next to the background colors must be light enough for contrast. (See Plate 14) With a light background, the darker values in your design must be used for contrast. (See Plate 15)

Remember, if a warm combination of colors is desired, use reds, yellows, and browns; while for a cold combination, use blues and greens. (See Plate 18)

Another idea is to use many shades of a color and then one accent color, as, for instance, a field of yellow daisies and a purple butterfly.

Applying Design to Canvas

Applying the design to canvas is made quite a simple matter by following a few basic rules. If the design must be counted out stitch by stitch, or a border plotted out so that the corners mesh right, it must be done on graph paper first. Otherwise, most designs are simply traced over an inked drawing onto the canvas.

Start with a good, simple, black-ink outline drawing on white paper or on tracing paper, that has been placed over a blank sheet of white paper. Even tan paper with an ink drawing won't show up under the canvas. The inked drawing should be simple—details can be added later when painting the canvas.

Be sure the design is centered leaving a two-inch border all around.

Be sure that the horizontal and vertical lines in the design line up with the horizontal and vertical lines of the canvas.

Tack canvas down over the design (on white covered board) and trace onto canvas with India waterproof ink. Allow ink to dry for about a half hour before painting.

Some people don't want to paint their canvas at all, and there is no reason to, if they know what colors and shades are wanted where. If, however, there is uncertainty about this, painting the canvas will help clarify the thinking and give sort of a preview of what the finished piece will look like. When using certain variety stitches it is advisable to paint in areas to be

Simple ink line drawing

Details added to painted canvas

stitched as canvas might show through. This is especially true of straight stitches such as brick, Hungarian and Parisian. Since acrylics dry very fast, color changes can be made right on the canvas in a matter of minutes; with oil it is necessary to wait much longer.

The design is on the canvas—now for the painting. Mix the oils or acrylics to the consistency of very light cream, apply paint gently but firmly, lightest shades and largest areas first. There is no need to paint in the background unless it is to be very dark, or unless brick stitch or another straight stitch is planned. If the holes get filled, lift canvas and blow the paint out, then thin paint a little more or use less paint. Practice a little on a canvas scrap before starting the magnum opus. Don't forget that the painted piece will hopefully be covered with wool. Not the painting, but the worked piece is to be the star. The painting is simply the guide, not the end result. Keep it neat and simple.

Paint a pale line around the design as a border, an inked line might show through the wool. Bind the edges with masking tape, or sew on bias tape. Allow paint to dry one hour for acrylics and at least twenty-four hours for oils. Start stitching.

Designs with Specific Stitches in Mind

The basic stitch of all canvas embroidery is, of course, the tent stitch. The complete mastery of this stitch, both the straight and the diagonal, is essential for all good work. The stitch should be even, should lie flatly against the material, and should be of the same tension. Working in a frame helps to do this. Half cross stitch which appears the same on the face of the work is not recommended. On mono-canvas, it will slip and, on any canvas, the back is not particularly firm.

Using tent stitch as the basic stitch, the design often may be enhanced by other stitches. They are easy to do and offer a pleasing diversion from working the tent. In fact, working the so-called "variety" stitches, is something like eating peanuts!

Making stitch samplers is a fine way to see how the stitches look "in person", as it were, and is a good reference tool. One such sampler is illustrated on page 52. It includes Oriental, chequer double cross, Byzantine, Ray, Turkey knot, Old Florentine, St. George and St. Andrew, diamond eyelet, double straight cross, Cushion, Satin, as well as Reverse Tent.

Many of these stitches make charming backgrounds and give a welcome relief from the ever present diagonal tent. Picture a fire-breathing dragon worked completely in tent stitch cavorting on a background of Jacquard. The use of the Jacquard stitch has added a new dimension to the work that would never have been there had tent stitch been used. Brick stitch is a very effective background which works up very quickly, while

Diagram 1. FROG

      A — Tent   **C** — Encroaching Gobelin (all leaves)
      B — French Knots   **D** — Mosaic

both Hungarian and Parisian are excellent, also, to name but a few. Backgrounds are fun to experiment with; there is always one specific stitch that is right for the piece being completed. Hunt around for it. Sometimes fitting the background stitch around the design proves a bit troublesome. Often a couple of rows of tent stitch all around the design is helpful. If 2 or 3 threads are used in working the background, as the design is approached use just 1 thread. This will often solve this dilemma.

In using stitches other than tent, care must be taken not to use too many. It is easy to get fascinated with a variety of stitches, but the resulting busyness is to be avoided. The following pages have many designs that have been planned to avoid this. All stitches specified in these designs are found listed alphabetically in the Stitch Charts in Chapter 9, p. 83.

Diagram 2. SANDPIPERS

 A — Smyrna Cross
 B — 2 rows Scotch
 C — 2 rows Mosaic
 D — Encroaching Oblique
 E — Tent (all birds)
 F — Brick over 3 holes (2 shades of brown)

Diagram 3. BUTTERFLY TWINS
A— Chequer
B— Southern Cross
C— Brick
D— Tent

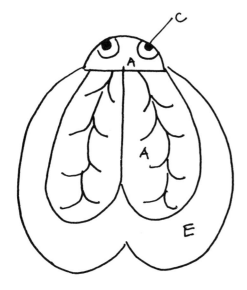

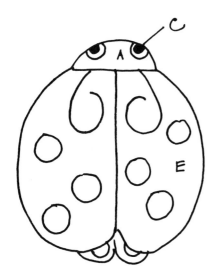
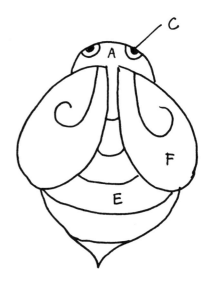

Diagram 4. BUGS

A — Tent
B — Smyrna Cross
C — French Knot
D — Parisian
E — Mosaic
F — Upright Cross

Diagram 5. BOW POCKETBOOK
A— Upright Cross
B— Tent
C— Parisian
D— Smyrna Cross (all centers)
E— Hungarian

Diagram 6. TULIP

A— Tent
B— Byzantine
C— French Knots
D — Encroaching Gobelin
E — Encroaching Oblique

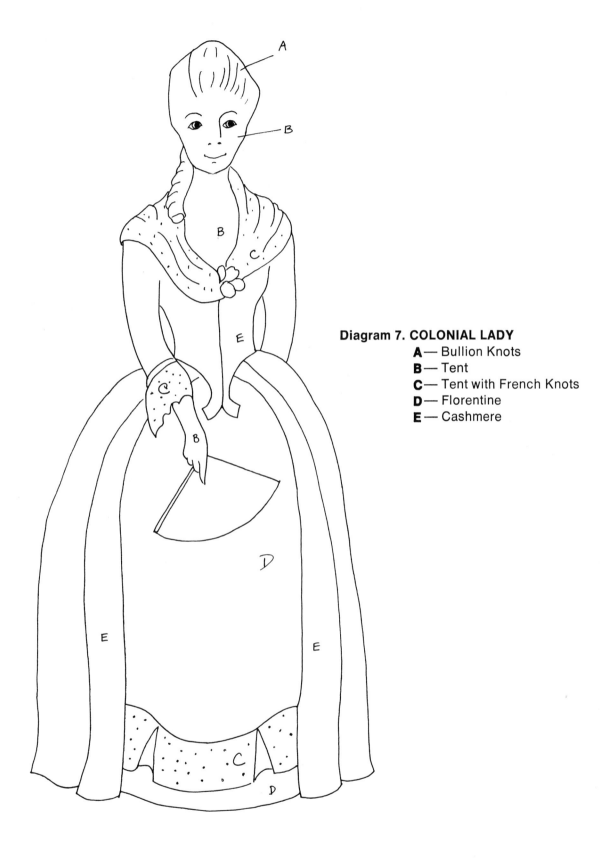

Diagram 7. COLONIAL LADY

A — Bullion Knots
B — Tent
C — Tent with French Knots
D — Florentine
E — Cashmere

Diagram 8. COUNTRY MOUSE

A — Smyrna Cross
B — Bargello
C — Tent (2 strands)
D — Tent (1 strand)
E — Turkey
F — Gobelin over 3 rows
G — Tent
H — Brick
I — Hungarian in 2 colors
J — Encroaching Gobelin

Diagram 9. CITY MOUSE

- **A** — Hungarian
- **B** — Brick
- **C** — Turkey
- **D** — Tent
- **E** — Encroaching Gobelin
- **F** — Smyrna Cross
- **G** — Kalem
- **H** — Parisian
- **I** — Gobelin
- **J** — Slanted Gobelin
- **K** — Upright Cross
- **L** — Shaded light to dark

Diagram 10. DAFFODILS

A — Tent
B — French Knots
C — Bargello
D — Encroaching Oblique
E — Brick

Diagram 11. MUSHROOM — FROG

A — Brick
B — Smyrna Cross
C — Tent
D — Turkey
E — Reverse Tent over 2 rows
F — Upright Cross

G — Jacquard
H — Milanese
I — Encroaching Gobelin
J — Overlay Running Stitch
Reverse Tent over 1 row
K — French Knots

Diagram 12. HERB POTS

A — French Knots
B — Tent
C — Scotch
D — Mosaic
E — Scotch

Diagram 13. TENNIS RACQUET COVER
A — Tent
B — Brick
C — Slanted Gobelin
D — Tent with Slanted Gobelin
E — Turkey
F — Upright Cross
G — Scotch

Diagram 14. GIRAFFE

A — Encroaching Gobelin
B — French Knot
C — Tent (leaves)
D — Mosaic (spots)
E — Brick
F — Tent
G — Tent

Diagram 15. LEAF CARD TABLE COVER

A — Diagonal
B — Reverse Tent
C — Byzantine
D — Cashmere
E — Hungarian
F — Oriental 1-3
G — Oriental 2-4

H — Parisian
I — Mosaic
J — Jacquard
K — Upright Cross
L — Tent (all small leaves)
M — Brick (background)
N — Scotch (all 4 borders)

Diagram 16. FISH

- **A** — Tent
- **B** — Gobelin (3 hole)
- **C** — Hungarian
- **D** — Leaf
- **E** — Long Armed Cross
- **F** — Upright Cross
- **G** — Byzantine
- **H** — Tent
- **I** — Tent

B

H

C

D

G

F

I

Diagram 17. GOLF PILLOW

    A— Tent (all figures)
    B — Brick (all backgrounds of figures)
    C — Bargello (all inside borders)
    D — Parisian (all areas outside circle)

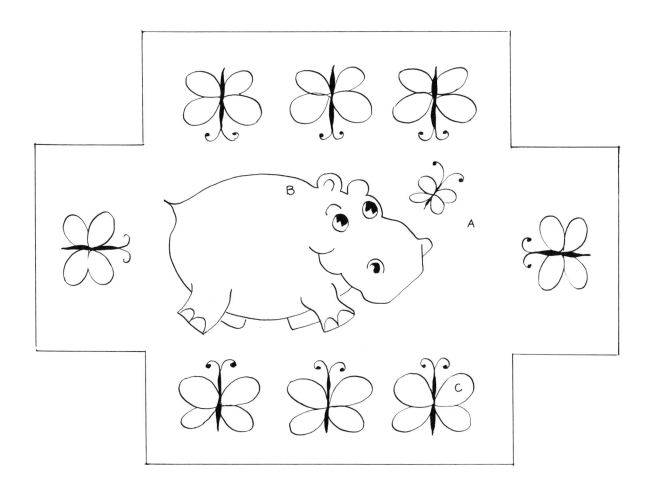

Diagram 18. HIPPO BRICK
A — Brick
B — Hungarian (details, Tent stitch)
C — Mosaic

Diagram 19. SAMPLER

A — Tent stitch
B — Kalem or Reverse Tent stitch
C — Diamond eyelet
D — Cross
E — Algerian eye and cross stitch
F — Old Florentine stitch
G — Turkey Knot stitch

H— Mosaic Stitch with tent stitch
I — Milanese stitch
J — Double Cross stitch
K— Byzantine stitch
L — Ray stitch
M— Shadow stitch
N — Flat stitch
O — Diamond

Inset with bee is done on 18 mesh canvas, woven in. Stitches are done in silk, using a combination of tent and symrna cross (See plate 11 and p. 25).

Designs for Special Occasions or Places

So far we have talked about the "how to" of needlepoint design, now we come to the "whys" and "what for." This field ranges from the purely decorative to the very personal. While it might be embarrassing to ask an artist to paint a picture to match a certain color scheme, and it would be prohibitively expensive to get a fabric house to design material just for one chair, and that unique present for Great-uncle Smedley's seventy-fifth birthday is hard to find, these are some of the "whys" and "what fors" of designing your own needlepoint.

The places and the occasions made memorable by a piece of needlepoint can be as varied as imagination itself. A mirror frame designed and worked by a whole family with their pets and enthusiasms as its motif could be a super project. (See Figure 14, p. 54) A chair seat copying a piece of Delft china or a wild flower rug designed for the garden club and stitched by its various members (See Plate 17) are other projects that are fun and can even be lucrative if put up for auction. Finding new ways to use needlepoint can also help get us out of the pillow rut, here are a few suggested patterns.

CARD TABLE

This card table cover pattern is for a standard 33 x 33-inch card table; measure your own table, however, to be sure of exact

Figure 14

measurements. (See Figure 15) There is no reason why the desired size cannot be inked right onto the canvas leaving 4 rows around the outside edge for turning under. A card table cover is a perfect place to use a backgammon board design or a chess or checkerboard pattern. Work out center playing area first, then add border. (See Plate 18) Any size canvas can be used however, since the piece is large, a 12″ or 10″ mesh is preferred.

Plate 1. Strawberry vine pocketbook
worked by Mrs. Anne Love (See p. 9)

Plate 2. Delphinium—Hummingbird mirror frame
worked by Mrs. John T. Hornblow (See p. 10)

Plate 3. Summer garden
worked by Mrs. Lucy Blum (See p. 10)

Plate 4. Lion cub
worked by Mrs. Wayne Wall (See jacket and p. 10)

Plate 5. Quail pillow with feather border
worked by Mrs. Francis Parsons (See p. 10)

Plate 6. Strawberries and Stripes (See p. 10)

Plate 7. Shell eyeglass case
worked by Mrs. Wayne Wall (See p. 17)

Plate 8. Color wheel (See p. 25)

Plate 9. Complementary colors (See p. 25)

Plate 10. Split complement (See p. 25)

Plate 11. Monochromatic mushroom sampler
worked by Muriel Baker (See p. 25)

Plate 12. Flowers with interesting triangle border
worked by Mrs. Ralph Burdick (See p. 26)

Plate 13. Fern frame in pale tones (See p. 26)

Plate 14. Tigers in the night; good use of dark background (See p. 28)

Plate 15. Panda; good contrast between
light background and figure (See p. 28)

Plate 16. Warm & cold color combinations, overlooked by interested cat (See p. 28)

Plate 17. Wildflower rug
worked by Farmington Connecticut Garden Club (See p. 53)

Plate 18. African animal backgammon board (See p. 54)

Plate 19. Rabbit hole Christmas stocking *worked by Mrs. Virginia Holshuh* (See p. 59)

Plate 20. Different designs for tennis racquets
worked by, left to right, Mrs. Frances Wasley, Miss Lucy Eyre,
Mrs. Wayne Wall (See p. 62)

Plate 21. Cummerbund, His favorite things
worked by Mrs. James Bell (See p. 65)

Plate 22. Non-Painted borders, made with fancy stitches
worked by Mrs. Muriel Baker (See p. 66)

Plate 23. Painted borders
worked by Mrs. Wayne Wall (See p. 67)

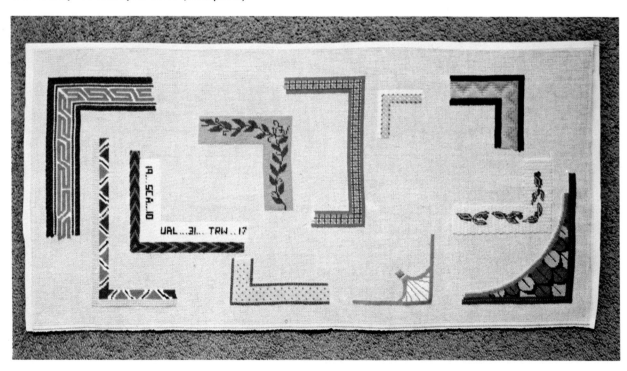

Plate 24. Framed sailboat
worked by Mrs. Francis Parsons (See p. 78)

Figure 15

CHAIRS, BENCHES, FOOTSTOOLS, VALANCES, HEADBOARDS

In measuring for chair seats, a paper pattern is not needed unless there is a curve to the front or back (See Figure 16) in which case a pattern is essential to figure correctly the curve in the design.

Figure 16

Measure a chair: from front to back
                 across the back edge
                 across the front edge
                 height of seat cushion in front, back, and side.
Allow an additional two inches for turning under edges.

If it is an arm chair or if the back sets into the seat, these indentations must also be measured. (See Figure 17)

The height of the seat cushion in some chairs is different from front to back; check measurements. (See Figure 18)

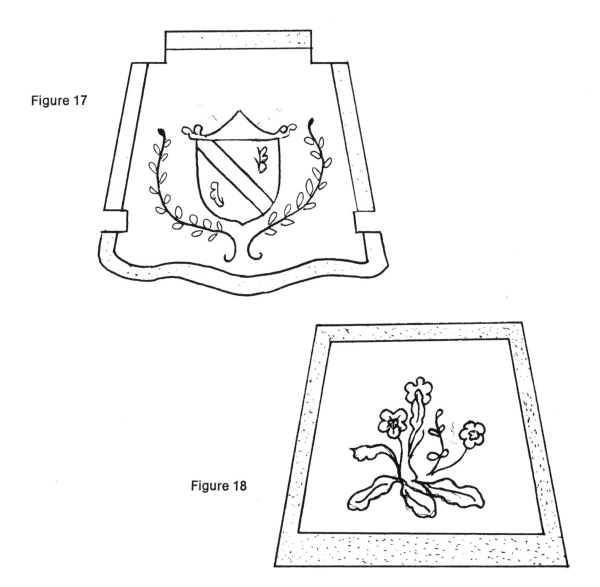

Figure 17

Figure 18

In designing for a winged chair or other upholstered pieces, it is wise to get an upholsterer to make a muslin pattern. Ask him to put a dotted line around it to show seam allowance.

When designing a footstool, bench, valances, or headboards, measure the same way as for a chair seat, using a paper pattern to show placement of any curves.

Chairs, headboards, etc. are best done on 12″ or 14″ mesh canvas, although a larger or smaller mesh can be used, depending on size and detail of the piece.

PICTURE OR MIRROR FRAMES

When measuring for a picture or mirror frame, decide first on the size of the center. The size of a mirror is not important, if the mirror is to be cut to size, but a picture frame center must be the right size for a photograph. Allow 3 worked rows around center and around outside edge for turn under.

A picture frame should not be busy as it detracts from the subject of the photograph, and this might be an excellent place to do a variety of stitches rather than a painted design.

Mirror frames can be as detailed or simple as desired. Decide on the width of frame area, then, as in the picture frame, add 3 worked rows for turn under around center edges and outside edges. On any type frame be sure the area to be cut out is centered. A mirror frame would lend itself to designs for special occasions or special interests. A wedding frame makes a lovely gift. Frames can be done in 18″, 16″, 14″ or 12″ mesh canvas, any larger mesh would have a tendency to ravel when it is being made up.

LUGGAGE STRAPS

Luggage straps are done in sets of two or three depending on the size and shape of the luggage rack. The set of three generally run 2½ x 22 inches. They can have the same pattern, the center strap may be different and the side straps similar, or all three straps different. If the latter, care must be taken to have a unifying idea, perhaps a son's sports or a family's hobbies. (See

Figure 19

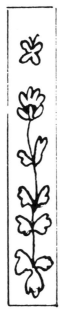

Figure 20

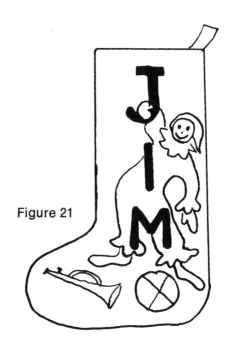

Figure 21

Figure 19) The set of two straps should have the same pattern. But if great care is given to the balance, two dissimilar designs can be used. (See Figure 20) Sets of two straps usually run 3½ x 22 inches. Remember to add 3 rows all around for turn under. When doing belts, wall hangings, or bell pulls the outline can be inked right onto the canvas after the size is decided upon. Any mesh canvas can be used for these projects.

CHRISTMAS STOCKING

A good size for a finished stocking is 16 x 13 inches. In planning the design do any lettering first and then plan additional design around it. (See Plate 19) Any mesh canvas, depending on design, can be used. (See Figure 21)

Figure 22

GLASSES CASE

Glasses cases can be made several ways.
1. Separate pieces of identical size and shape for front and back. (See Figure 22) Make sure the edges, if curved, are exact, they should be counted out on graph paper. The sides should measure 3½ x 6½ inches.
2. One long strip with a continuous design that is folded in half when finished. The strip should measure 3½ x 13 inches.
3. On a square design, that is folded down the center like a book, (See Figure 23) should measure 6¾ x 6½ inches.

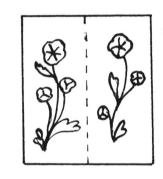

Figure 23

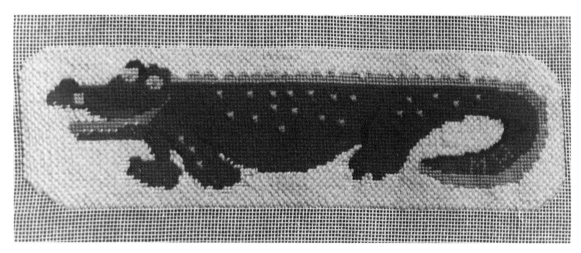

Continuous design for folded glasses case

These measurements are for standard size glasses and any mesh up to 12 can be used. If the design is for reading glasses or half glasses, the second or third pattern is best, and as it will be a small design, 18 or 16 inch mesh canvas is preferred. Measure the glasses, add ½ inch on each side and ¼ inch on each end for the pattern size.

If the design is to be large for sun glasses, the case and pattern will be larger, and 12 or 14 inch mesh canvas can easily be used. Any of the three patterns will do, simply measure the sun glasses and add ½ inch to top and sides of design.

BRICK DOORSTOP

Since bricks vary in size, the first step in designing would be to measure the specific brick to be used. The top and sides of the brick should be padded before mounting the worked canvas, so this must be considered.

Measure the width and length of the top, and the height and length of all four sides. Allow 6 rows all around outside edges for finishing and padding allowance. Make sure that the sides fold down on the same row of canvas all the way around.

Count rows on all four sides to make sure they are even. Plan the design so that it is well contained within the top of the brick, unless, of course, it is an all over design. Remember, a brick is seen mainly from the top. As one side is against the door, the main concern should be the top and three sides. Perhaps the date and three initials could be placed on the fourth side. 10 inch, 12 inch or 14 inch mesh is suitable for a brick. (See Figure 24)

Figure 24

Hippo is safe distance from border edge

TENNIS RACKET COVER

In making a tennis racket pattern it is important to know if the racket is a metal or wooden one; metal rackets are rounder and smaller. Place the racket on a piece of white paper and trace around it. Add 1½ inches all around tracing for seam allowance. Be sure the design does not come closer than 1¾ inch from outside edge, unless it is an all over design. (See Plate 21) Any mesh canvas is suitable for a tennis racket cover.

SCISSORS CASE

A scissors case is designed in one piece then, after stitching, is folded on the diagonal to form a wedge-shaped case. Either an all over pattern or a different design and back is nice. This is a small piece so an 18" or 16" mesh canvas should be used. (See Figure 25)

Figure 25

DIRECTOR'S CHAIR

A standard wooden director's chair is 15½ x 18 inches for the seat and 7 x 42½ inches for the back, and should be stitched in one long piece then joined at center back or on one side; plan the design carefully so that the joining ends will meet correctly. (See Figure 26) If a non-standard director's chair is being used, measure seat width and length, add ½ inch all around for turn under plus enough allowance to go over side bars and under the seat of chair. (See Figure 27) Measure the back all the way

Figure 26

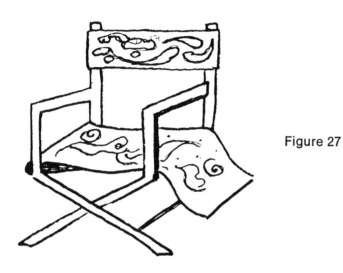

Figure 27

around and add ½ inch on sides and end for turn under. Any mesh canvas is good for director's chairs, number 12, 10, or larger being the easiest for so large an undertaking.

RUGS

Whole books have been written on this subject, but here we will attempt to give the basics and some important tips. If the width of the rug is to be larger than 3 feet, or if the rug can be done in small portions, the design should be done in squares or long strips. Squares, of course, are easiest to manage.

If a small area rug is wanted, 3 x 5 feet is an excellent size, and should be done on a good floor frame. When doing a rug in squares or strips, it is important to cut the pieces from the same roll of canvas. In this way the warp and weft, which vary from roll to roll, will be the same size, thus insuring the same stitch size. Also, make sure that the canvas runs the same direction on all strips or squares. A good system to follow is to cut the squares or strips all at once, bind them, and mark the right upper corner.

Counting holes of each square is essential to be sure they are all the exact size. If a border around each square is to be used, the inner border is half the width of the outside border. (See Figure 28)

When deciding on the design for a rug here are a few points to remember. When using large rug canvas or even 10″ mesh, keep the design large and simple, with areas of flat color, to be very effective. If more intricacy is wanted, a smaller mesh canvas is indicated, but still, areas with two to three tones of a color and simple designs are best.

Rugs are large, time-consuming pieces, so plan well before beginning and realize the length of time that will be involved. Rugs are wonderful group projects.

Figure 28

CUMMERBUND

Another excellent pattern that would make a successful special occasion present is a man's cummerbund. (See Plate 20) The center part should measure 4½ x 29 inches, and should curve down on each end to 3 inches. These are finished measurements so stitch a couple of extra rows all around for turn under; this is the worked area, the back is made of elastic or fabric. (See Figure 29)

Figure 29

Initials, Borders, and Boxing

Each piece of embroidery that is completed should be marked with name or initials and date of completion. Who knows what museum curator two hundred years from now will be exclaiming over the work and saying wistfully, "If only we knew who worked this and the exact date!" Do not pass up this chance for immortality.

A set of marking initials is, therefore, included—be sure to use them. Also included are sets of distinctive initials for marking the backs of handbags, pillows, and the like. They are also decorative enough to stand alone and would make charming small pillows or bags. (See Figures 30, 31, 32, & 33, p. 68-73)

Many a weak design has been saved by a good border. But a border is not something to be added after the design has been completed and it seems to need a little something else. A border should be a carefully thought-out part of any design. Combinations of stitches make attractive borders. (See Plate 23) Try a row of Smyrna Cross, 2 rows of Cashmere, and another row of Smyrna, with the corners in Leviathan. Stunning! Or try 6-row Herringbone, each row in a different color. Small Florentine patterns, with the corners carefully mitered make beautiful borders. Place Southern cross in all four corners and use Scotch, Greek, and William and Mary in consecutive rows. Try Jacquard, mitering the corners. Try William and Mary using it as indicated in the sampler. To miter the corners, simply draw a diagonal line through the width of the border, and then start in the center of each side and work toward this diagonal line. (See Figure 34, p. 73) Experiment, there is no end to the delightful combination of stitches that can be used for a border.

Some borders are painted on the canvas along with the design. The large border sampler (See Plate 22) shows many examples of this type. The border of feathers is especially good for bird designs but could be used successfully with any woodland scene. The combination of Parisian and tent stitch is a pleasing one in the holly berry design, and Gobelin combined with fern and tent offers a distinctive border that would improve a weak design immensely. And, of course, the old reliable tent stitch can be used in so many different ways, to make polka dots, checks, strips, Greek keys, and even the stock market report. A painted border should be designed at the same time as the center, so it will be an integral part of the whole design.

Traditionally, boxing has used plain tent stitch and has been an endless exercise for those who did it. But boxing need not be dreary. Variety stitches, such as Hungarian, Parisian, Greek, Cashmere and Smyrna Cross, to name but a few, make excellent boxing stitches. And very often some motif from the design is used which is always very pleasing.

Again, experiment, use imagination, and do not think that boxing must be just tent. Some of the borders illustrated would make lovely and distinctive boxings.

All stitches mentioned in this chapter are found listed alphabetically in the Stitch Charts in Chapter 9, p. 83.

Figure 30   **FLOWER ALPHABET**

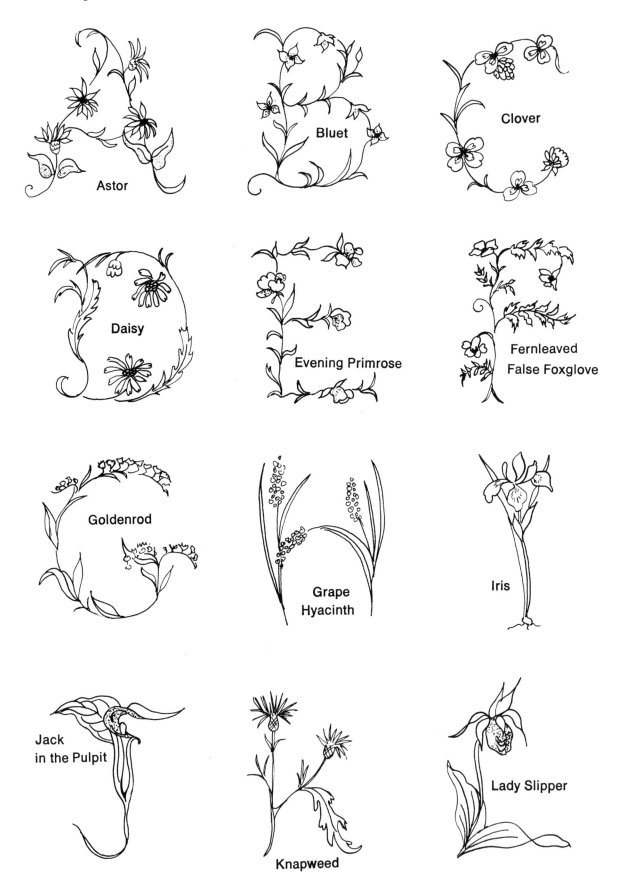

Astor

Bluet

Clover

Daisy

Evening Primrose

Fernleaved
False Foxglove

Goldenrod

Grape
Hyacinth

Iris

Jack
in the Pulpit

Knapweed

Lady Slipper

Morning Glory

Nettle

Orchid

Pinesap

Queen Anne's Lace

Rose (Pasture)

Strawberry

Trillium

Utricularia Intermedia
(Flatleaved Bladderwort)

Venus Looking Glass

Woodsorrels
(Tall Yellow Wood Sorrel)

Xanthoxalis Cymosa

Yarrow

Zinnia

Figure 31   **ANIMAL ALPHABET**

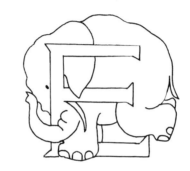

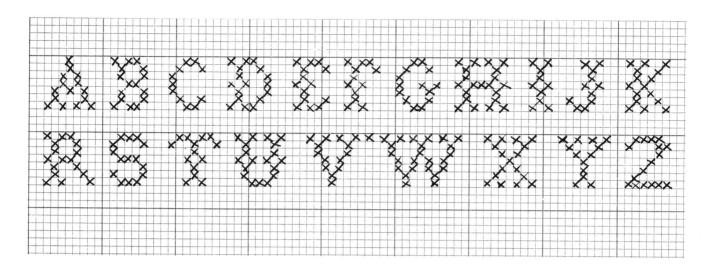

Figure 32   **BLOCK ALPHABET**

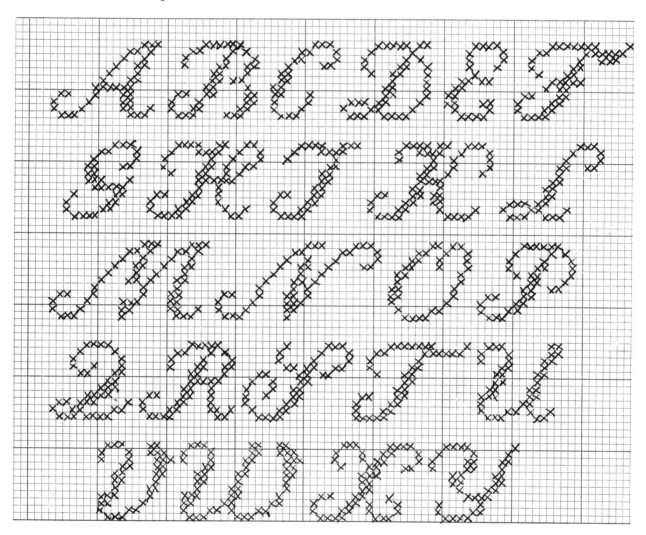

Figure 33   **SCRIPT ALPHABET**

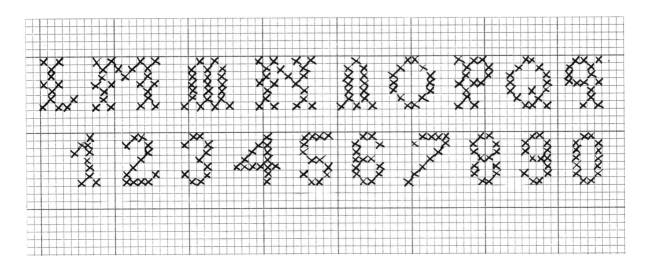

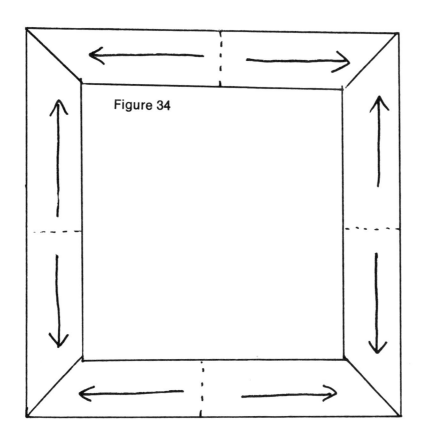

Figure 34

Mounting

Mounting your own needlepoint after completion is a project in itself. As in all the phases of designing and stitching, the greatest care should be taken, and the best materials and methods used. It is sad to see a lovely piece of needlepoint ruined by a careless mounting job. Many excellent professional mounters are available who, for the most part, are fairly expensive but well worth the money when compared with a ruined piece of work.

You can do your own mounting if you have average sewing skills, follow directions, and take your time. The exceptions are mounting leather goods and some upholstered pieces.

BLOCKING

The first step is to wash and block the finished piece to restore it to shape and make it clean and pliable. Equipment needed:

Brown paper

T square

Finishing nails—copper or rust proof bought by the box at a hardware store

Hammer

Large piece of plywood—wall board or floor underlay will do; all available at a lumber yard or for a small piece the good old bread board

Trace the original shape of the needlepoint onto a piece of brown paper, using the T square to make sure the corners are true. Cover the board with the brown paper with the tracing on it.

If the color fastness of the paint and wool are assured (a reputable yarn and a good brand of paint are safe), wash gently in cool water and a good wool soap. If in doubt about the color fastness of the materials, wash in cold salt water and do not rinse. Roll in a bath towel, and squeeze moisture out the way you would a good sweater.

While still damp, tack face up onto covered board, stretching the canvas as it is tacked so that it meets the traced dimensions on the brown paper. In some cases a bit of elbow grease must be used.

Do not tack into worked area, but into unworked canvas about ½ inch away from and all around worked area.

Allow to dry completely.

Remove tacks.

Mounting instructions for all the patterns in this book follow. If other projects are being undertaken, and there is doubt about how to mount them, consult a seamstress or upholsterer before beginning.

CARD TABLE COVER

Cut a piece of pretty soft material, cotton, linen or a blend, to the exact dimensions used to make needlepoint pattern. Cut eight, 1-inch wide grosgrain ribbons 6 inches long for the corners, or cut four pieces of ½-inch elastic 6 inches long. (See Figure 35) Baste material to needlepoint pattern facing. Be sure

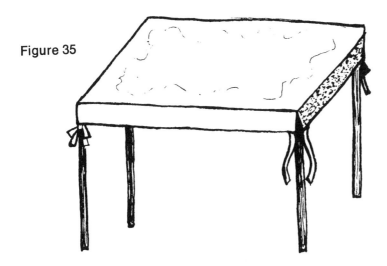

Figure 35

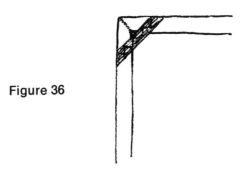

Figure 36

to sew 2 rows in from edge of needlepoint. If using ribbons for ties, baste two in each corner. Carefully stitch three sides on machine, making sure to stay in the same needlepoint row all around. Trim unstitched canvas to ¼ inch of worked area. Turn right side out like a large pillow case, steam press, and finish fourth side by hand. If not using ribbons to tie corners, stitch each of the four corners together and sew elastic across them. (See Figure 36)

CHAIRS

A slip chair seat or footstool can be mounted over existing fabric if the fabric is in good condition. It should not be mounted over leather or vinyl. Muslin is preferred.

Cut unworked canvas within ½ inch of worked area. Machine stitch, using zigzag stitch, all around worked area. Center design on seat, turn bottom up, with canvas held in place and tack in four places on bottom of seat to hold.

Fold corners in neatly and tack. (See Figure 37)

Pull rest of canvas very taut and tack all around into the worked area. Do not use staples as they can rust and damage the canvas. Rug tacks are good to use or the copper tacks used for blocking.

Figure 37

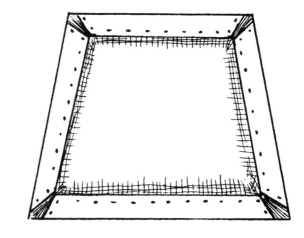

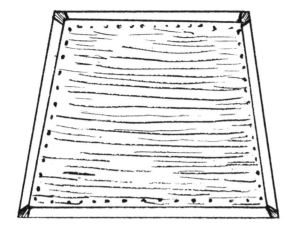

Figure 38

Once the needlepoint is tacked very securely on the seat bottom, cover bottom with black muslin to ¼ inch of edge. (See Figure 38)

When mounting a valance or headboard, be sure that they are padded and covered with muslin or good material before beginning. Mount in same way as slip seat, covering finished back with black muslin. Two people would be advisable for this job.

If slip chair seat has a curve center design, turn over and tack in four places to hold design in place. Start with center of curve, work first out to one side, then the other, making a small series of tucks on the inner curves and tacking them down. (See Figure 39) Keep tuck sizes even. Remember to tack into worked canvas. Keep canvas taut all around and finish tacking other sides. If the seat, footstool, etc., has to be upholstered, take it to a professional, preferably one who has worked with needlepoint before.

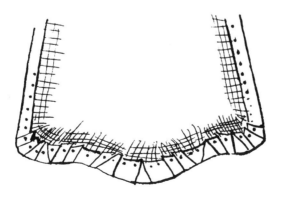

Figure 39

LUGGAGE STRAPS

Back the wall hangings, bell pulls, luggage straps, and belts with some pliable but stoutly woven materials; linen, cotton, or grosgrain are all used. A pretty print lining can sometimes add to the charm of the completed piece.

Place needlepoint and fabric together, pattern to pattern. Stitch along three sides, making sure to stay in same row all the way around, stitching 2 rows in on worked needlepoint is usual. Cut unworked canvas ¼ inch from worked area. Turn right side out, press with steam iron, hand sew fourth side.

Tack luggage straps to underside of rack with large-headed tacks, not thumb tacks.

FRAMING PICTURES

The easiest way to frame a design as a picture is to buy artist canvas stretchers at an art supply store. They come in all sizes. Assemble the stretchers and stretch the needlepoint over them as a painter would his canvas; start with a tack in the center of each side, pull very taut and tack all around the stretcher top, bottom and sides. Tack into worked area. (See Figure 40) A frame can now be bought or custom made for the picture; the aluminum frames that come in various sizes are excellent for needlepoint. (See Plate 24)

Figure 40

It is advisable to have a worked mirror frame or a picture frame mounted professionally. Many good framing stores will do it, but shop around for one that has done needlepoint before.

STOCKING

Cut two pieces of felt with pinking shears using exact pattern that was used for the needlepoint design. Cut one piece of felt 4½ inches long x 1 inch wide. Use a good quality felt. Baste worked needlepoint, face inward, to one piece of felt, leaving top open. Stitch on machine making sure to stay in same row where possible. Clip unworked canvas ¼ inch from worked area. Turn right side out, finish top by hand. Stitch needlepoint and backing to second piece of felt, keep stitching in same rows. Sew loop made from felt strip into top corner opposite toe of stocking. Fill with goodies.

GLASSES CASES

A pretty, soft material should be chosen as lining for a glasses case. Cut fabric to exactly the same measurements as pattern used for the design. Place needlepoint and fabric face-to-face and baste around three sides. Sew around three sides two rows in, being sure to stay along same row unless it curves. Turn inside out and finish fourth side by hand. Back is then sewn to front or side-to-side either with invisible plastic thread or with a hand done whipping with wool that matches the needlepoint; again care must be taken to stay in same row when whipping; a double strand of wool makes a neat whipped edge. (See Figure 41)

Figure 41

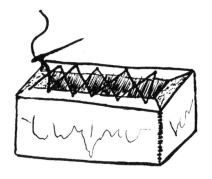

Figure 42

BRICK DOOR STOP

Measure brick carefully, a brick smaller than the design is necessary to allow for padding. Wrap brick in foam rubber, cotton batting, old soft towels, anything that will make a soft padding to keep edges of brick from cutting through needlepoint. The top often is padded more than the sides. Cover neatly with muslin to hold padding in place.

Sew corners of needlepoint together on machine, being sure to stay in the same row. Slip on padded brick. Use lacing stitches to hold needlepoint in place. (See Figure 42) Trim unworked canvas to ¼ inch of worked area. Hand stitch a piece of dark, strong fabric on bottom.

TENNIS RACKET COVER

½ yard of material, usually canvas
11-inch metal zipper
1½ yards of piping

Cut two pieces of material using exact dimension of your needlepoint design pattern. Trim unworked canvas to ¼ inch from worked area. Put needlepoint face down on one piece of material, baste. Machine stitch together in 2 rows, leaving neck and 3 inches open at lower edge. Turn right side out, steam press, and finish lower edges by hand.

Stitch piping to other piece of material, measure to be sure that the two pieces of material are the same size. Baste both sides together. Put in zipper leaving ½ inch at bottom neck for turn under. Machine stitch both sides together. Turn under bottom hem, press, and hand stitch.

SCISSORS CASE

The scissors case should be lined exactly as a glasses case using a pretty, soft material; use the needlepoint pattern to cut the lining. Then fold on the diagonal, and the two sides and small end sewn together with invisible plastic thread or whipped closed with matching needlepoint wool. The large end is left open for the scissors.

DIRECTOR'S CHAIR

A standard director's chair is mounted in the following way. Take the canvas seat that comes with the chair, take the worked needlepoint, cut ¼ inch around unworked area, fold under all around so that it fits exactly the seat area of the director's chair inside the arms. Baste, steam, and machine stitch needlepoint and canvas together all around, making sure to stitch in same rows all around. To mount the back, turn under all sides of needlepoint, clip excess ¼ inch from worked area, baste, and steam flat. Turn inside out, join the two ends and stitch. Turn right side out, place around wooden back uprights. Hand stitch front to back, top and bottom. (See Figure 43)

Figure 43

RUGS

If rugs are to be mounted at home, a book on rug mounting should be obtained from a library, better still, they should be mounted professionally.

CUMMERBUND

A cummerbund should be lined in some soft, silky fabric; satin is perfect. Place needlepoint face-to-face with lining, baste around outside edges 2 rows in on needlepoint, leave ends open and cut excess canvas ¼ inch from worked area. Stitch on machine. Turn right side out. Measure waist, cut elastic to fit snugly. The needlepoint area is 29 inches so figure out the remaining inches needed. Cut a piece of 3-inch black elastic to needed measurement, leaving ½ inch on end to be inserted in cummerbund. On one end, insert 3-inch black elastic, turn under worked edge, hand stitch edge and elastic together. On other end of elastic put a row of three eyes. (See Figure 44) Finish end of elastic with black seam binding. Turn under unfinished end of cummerbund, stitch by hand, and sew three hooks to that end.

Figure 44

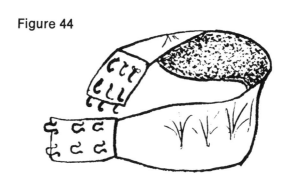

Diagrams of Stitches

On the following pages you will find diagrams of stitches required to do all the designs in this book. They are in alphabetical order.

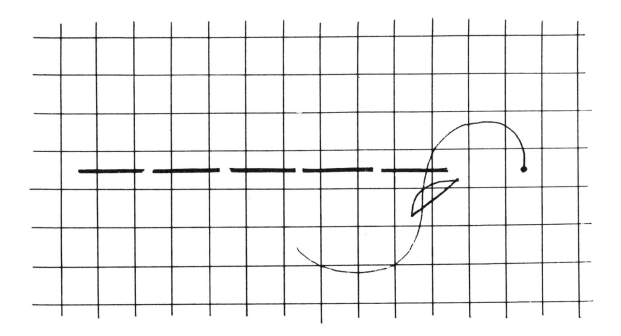

Back Stitch. This simple stitch is used to fill in any space where the canvas shows.

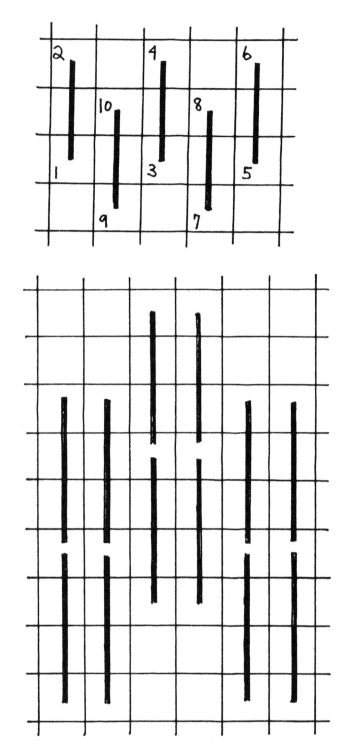

Brick Stitch. It works up quickly over as many holes as desired, but best not to exceed four.

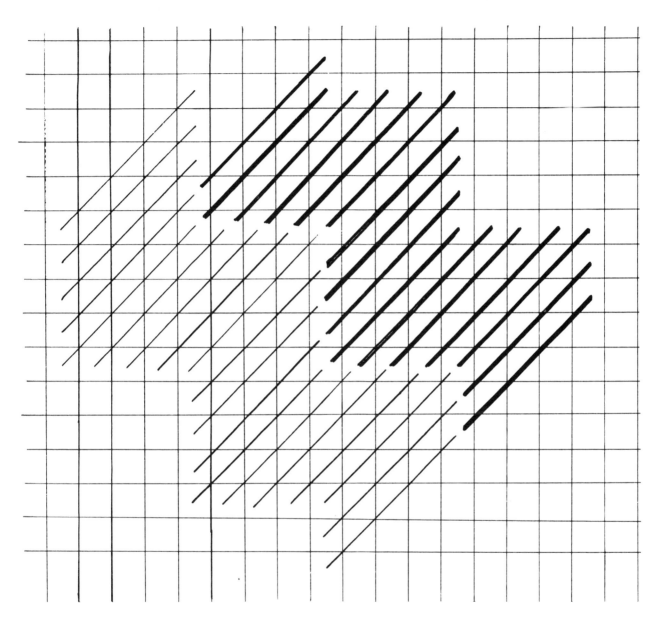

Byzantine Stitch. It is worked in a series of slant-
ing stitches in a zigzag pattern.

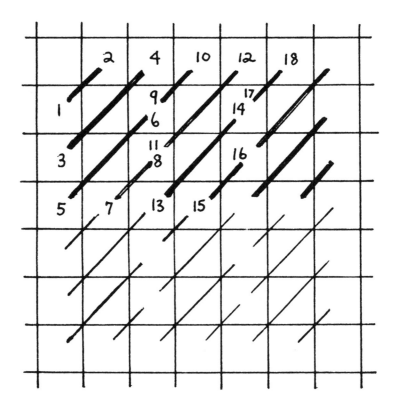

Cashmere Stitch. A variant of the Mosaic stitch. (p. 102) It makes a nice background and moves along quickly.

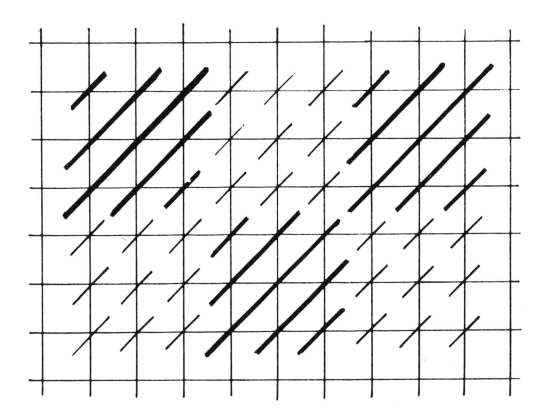

Chequer Stitch. The flat stitch alternates with the tent stitch. Do the flat stitch, skipping the tent and fill in later with the tent stitch.

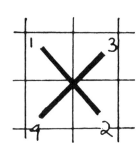

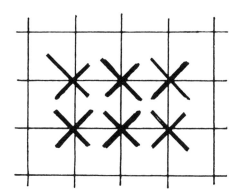

Cross Stitch. The upper stitch slopes from top right to bottom left, and its direction should remain the same. Each cross should be completed before going on to the next.

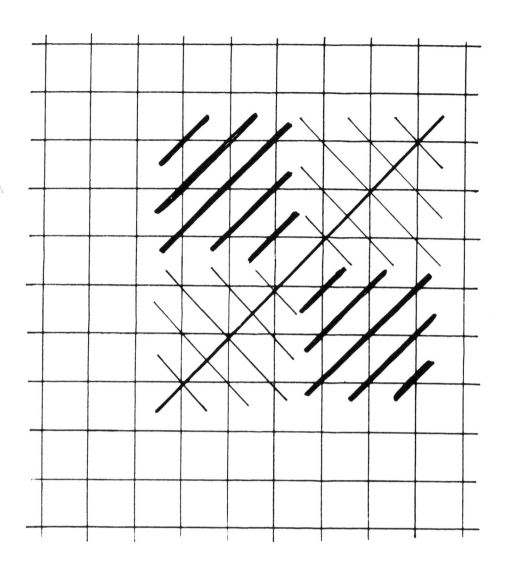

Cushion Stitch. Most interesting worked in two shades. Two "sets" of diagonal stitches forming stitches forming little squares are worked as usual. The other "set" is worked over a laid thread.

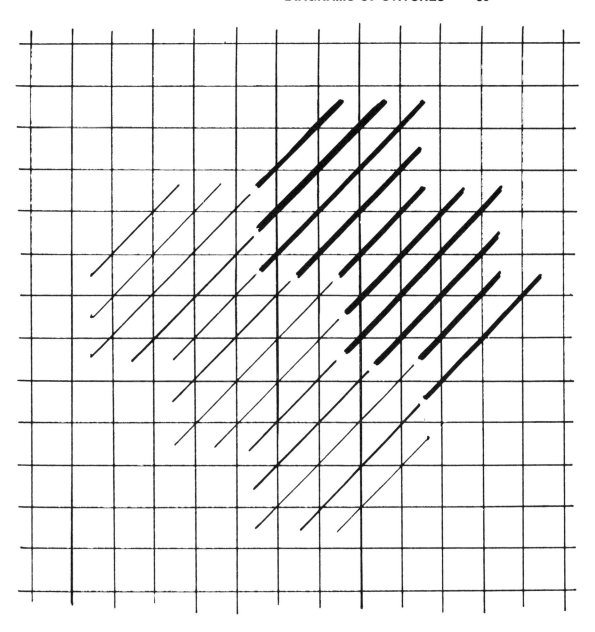

Diagonal Stitch. This gives the effect of brocade in backgrounds. May be worked in one or two shades or colors depending on the desired effect.

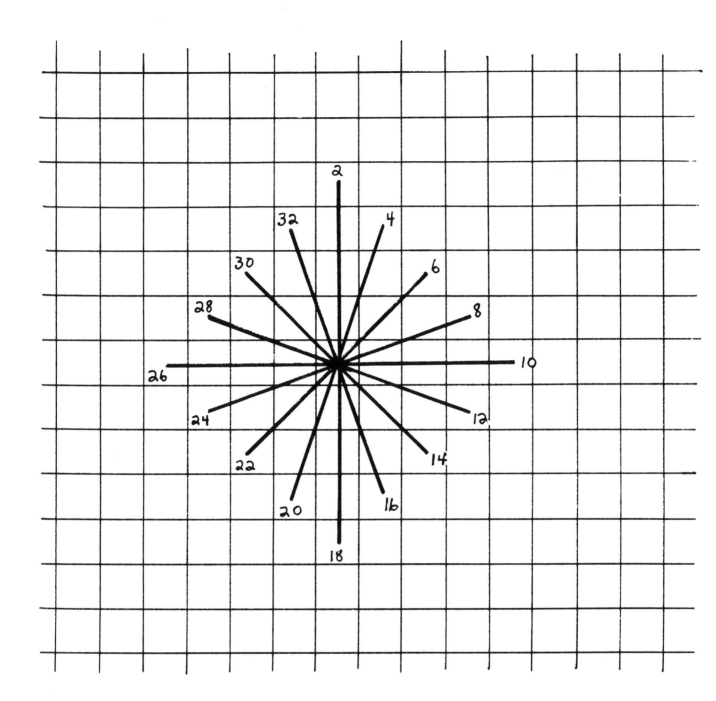

Diamond Eyelet Stitch. Odd numbers starting with 1 are down through center hole. Since canvas will show around the edges of the completed stitch, a running stitch or a back stitch may be used as an outline.

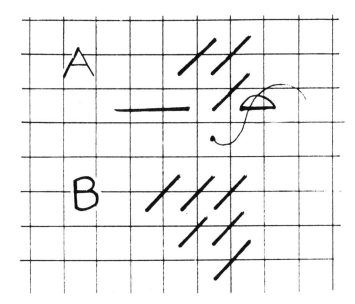

going up

Diagonal Tent Stitch. A good background stitch. On the "going up" sequence the needle is horizontal as shown on **A. B** shows how work appears when that sequence is completed. On the "going down" sequence the needle is in the vertical position as in **C. D** shows "going down" sequence completed.

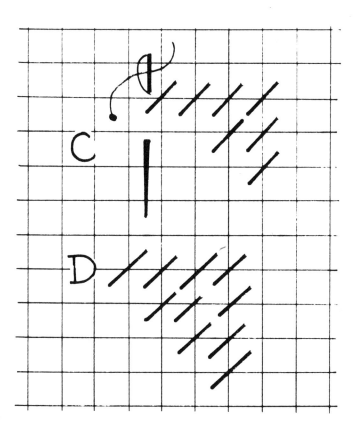

going down

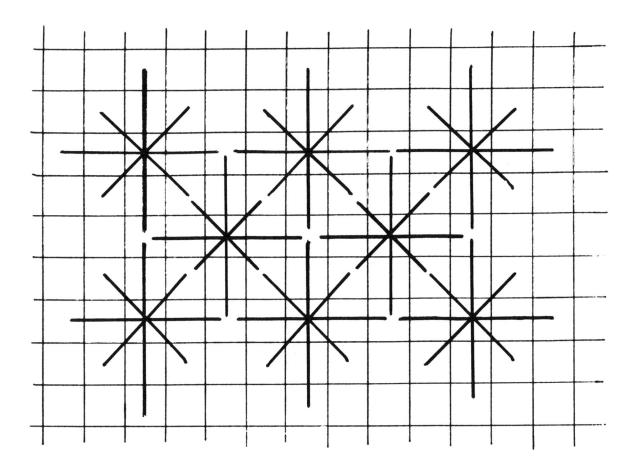

Double Cross Stitch. A combination stitch using a
large stitch and a small upright cross.

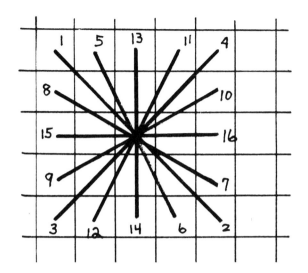

Double Leviathan. An excellent border stitch.

Triple Leviathan Stitches. Triple leviathan can only be used as an accent.

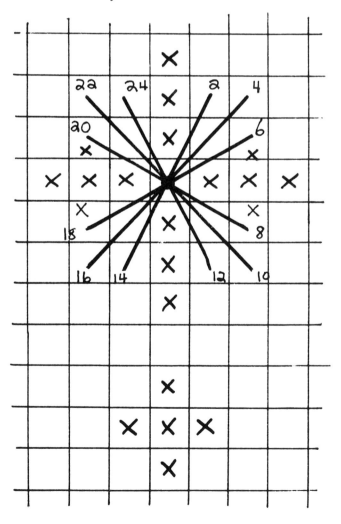

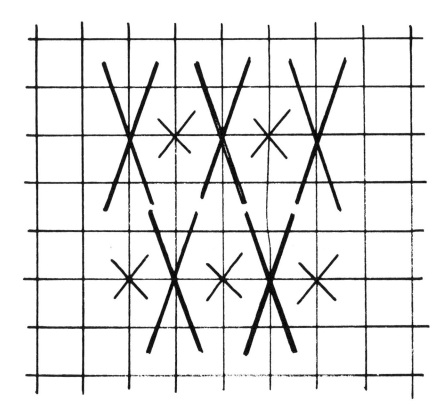

Double Straight Cross Stitch. Heavier in appearance than the upright cross. A neat, crisp stitch which is fun to use.

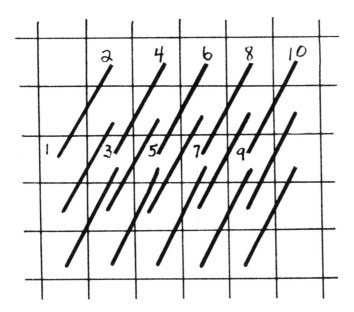

Encroaching Gobelin Stitch. A smooth textured stitch, good for shading as well as background. Worked up three holes and over one. It tends to pull out of shape and is best worked on a frame.

Encroaching Oblique Stitch. This stitch is worked in rows from left to right. Make each stitch by going ahead over 4 mesh and down over 1 mesh. Move back under 2 mesh and up under 1 mesh to find the starting hole for the next stitch.

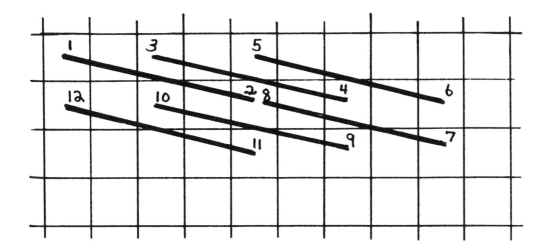

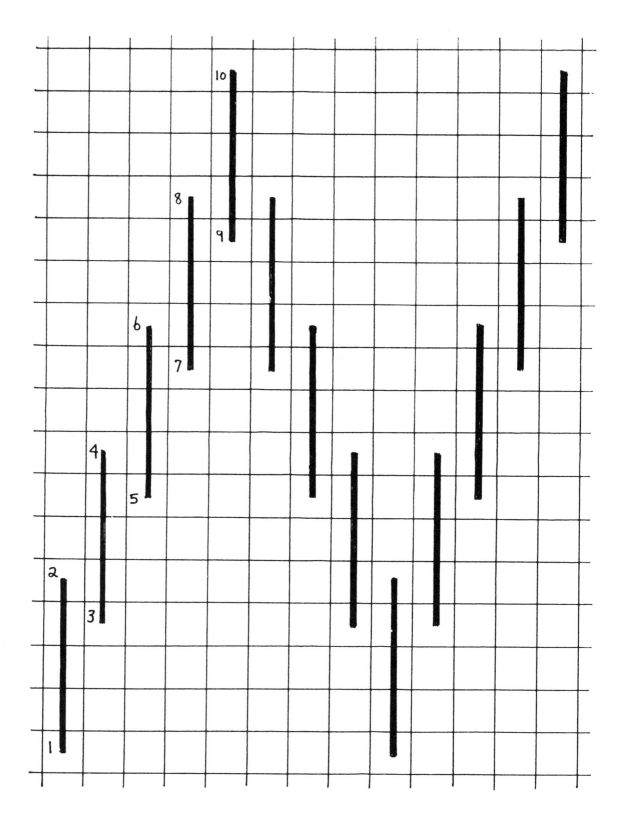

Florentine. One of the classic designs. There are many variations. Can be done in coordinated colors or in all one family of color.

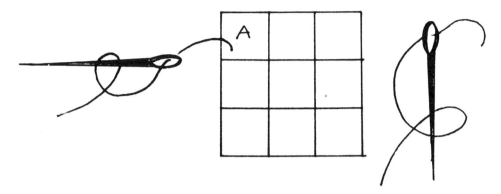

French Knot Stitch. Bring needle up at **A.** Twist thread once around the needle, holding wool flat to the left of **A.** While still keeping wool taut, put needle back down into **A.** Pull until it fits closely but not too tightly.

Gobelin Stitch. This stitch is likely to show the background of canvas, so it is advisable to paint the canvas the color of the yarn to be used.

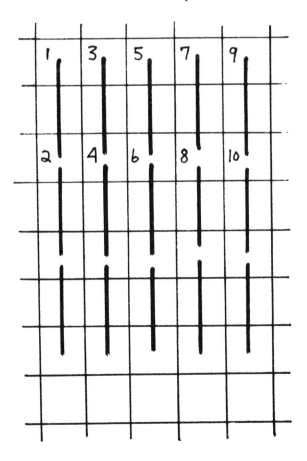

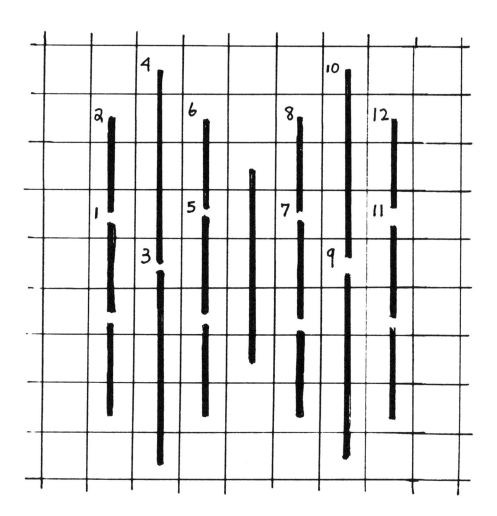

Hungarian Stitch. This can be done in two colors. It is worked over three holes, five holes, three holes, omitting a row, then 3-5-3 again. The next row of stitches fits up between the first, with the short stitches under the short stitches.

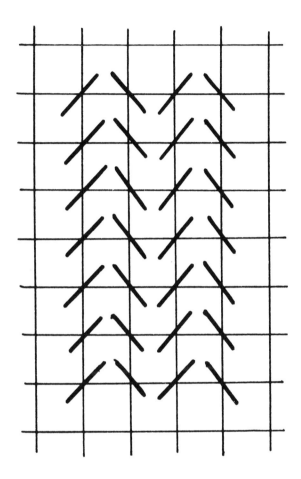

Kalem or Reverse Tent Stitch. An excellent stitch when stripes are indicated. Good worked in two shades of the same color.

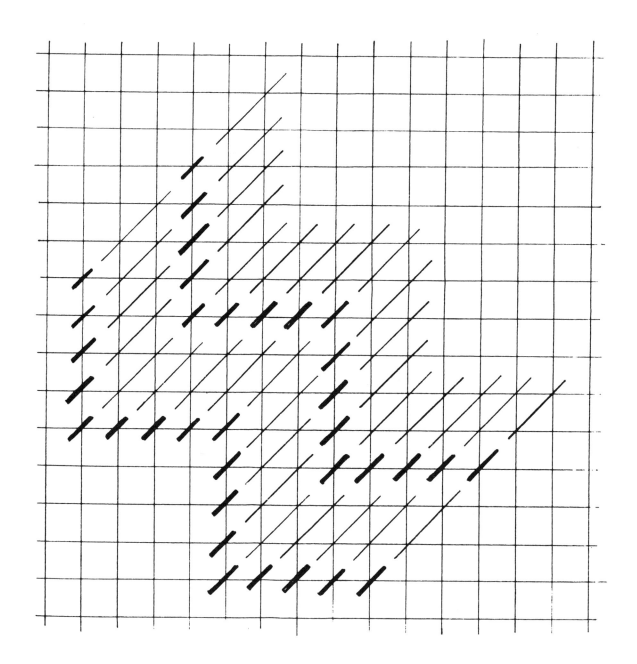

Jacquard Stitch. A useful pattern stitch. Can be worked in two colors giving a very trim appearance.

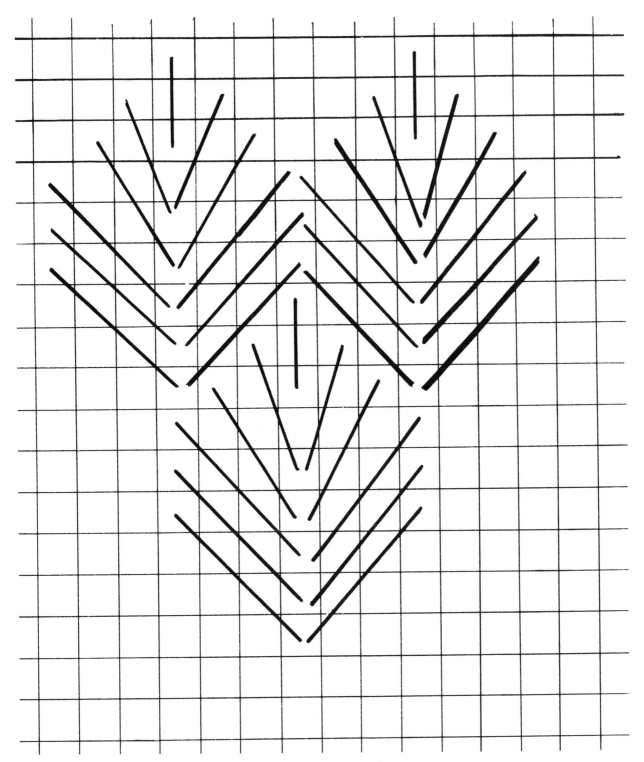

Leaf Stitch. Makes a beautiful border. Can be made larger or smaller by adding or subtracting the number of stitches. A center vein can be added and even a stem if desired.

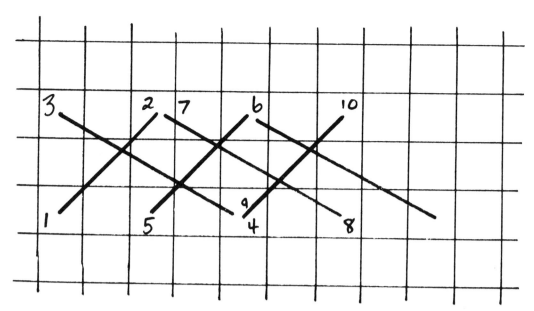

Long-Armed Cross Stitch. One cross is up three holes and over three holes. The other is up three holes and over five. Often found in rugs.

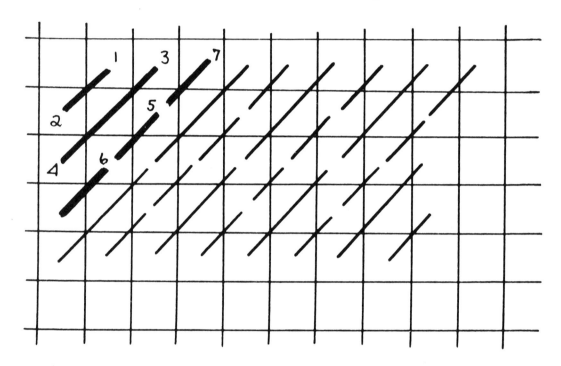

Mosaic Stitch. This is a good background stitch when done in monochrome and used in combination with the tent stitch. Many combinations of shades give variety to the design. Bring needle up on the odd numbers, down on the even.

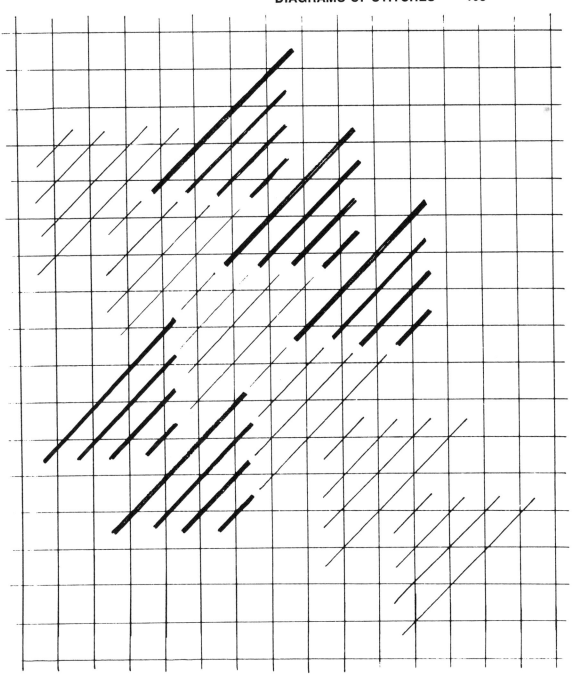

Milanese Stitch. Best worked in sharply contrasting shades. Makes tiny Christmas tree-like figures.

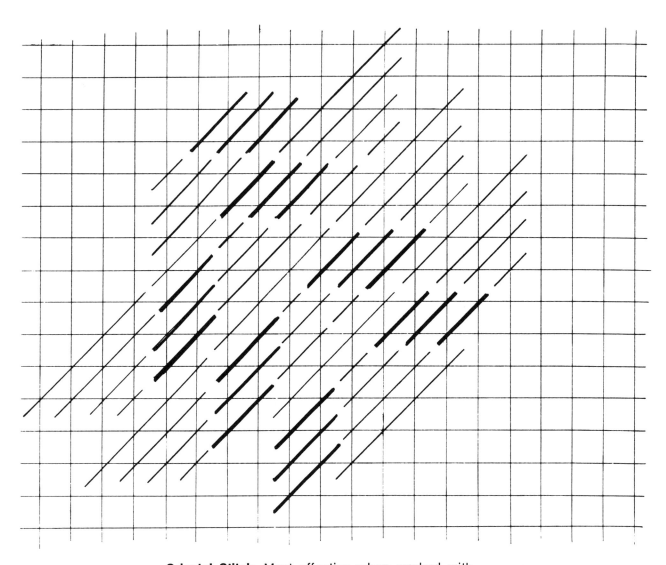

Oriental Stitch. Most effective when worked with strong contrasts. A good pattern stitch or as background for a plain design.

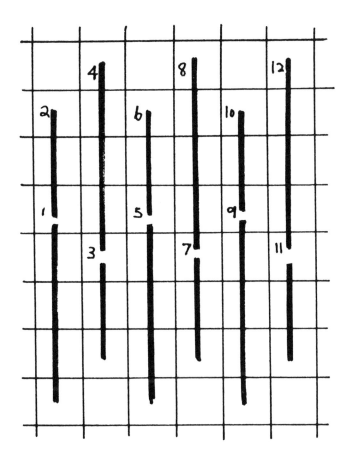

Parisian Stitch. Quick to work up. An upright stitch done over three holes, five holes, three holes, alternately. The long stitch is always under the short stitch. Effective in two colors.

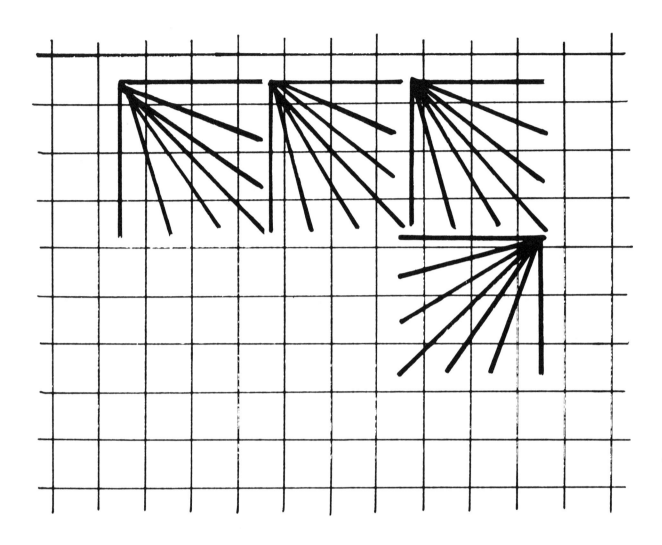

Ray Stitch. This may be done in either direction as shown. Also one row can be set in one direction, the next in the other direction. Not often seen but can make an interesting border.

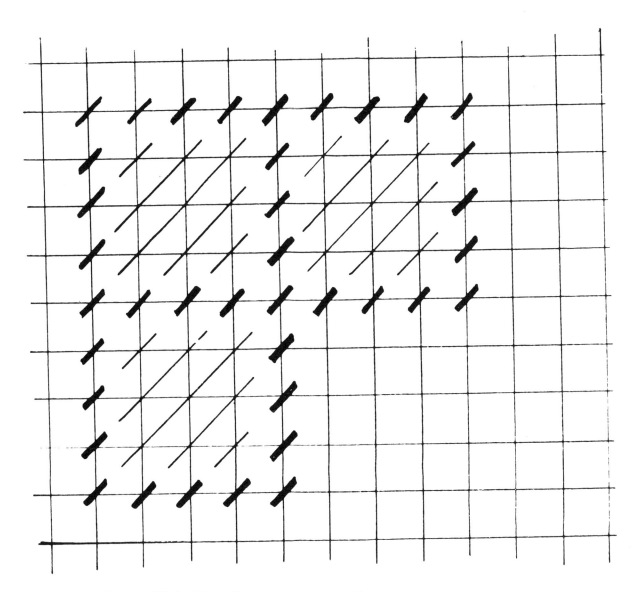

Scotch Stitch. This stitch has many variations and is most versatile. Can make an interesting background.

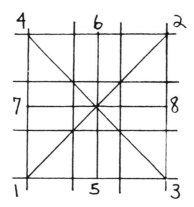

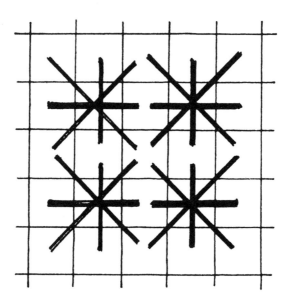

Smyrna Cross Stitch. This is a double cross worked over three holes of canvas each way. First a diagonal cross, than an upright cross over it.

4	12	20	28	36	29	21	13	5	2
7									10
15									18
23									26
31									34
30									35
22									27
14									19
6									11
1	9	17	25	33	32	24	16	8	3

Southern Cross Stitch. Bring needle up on odd numbers, go down on even numbers.

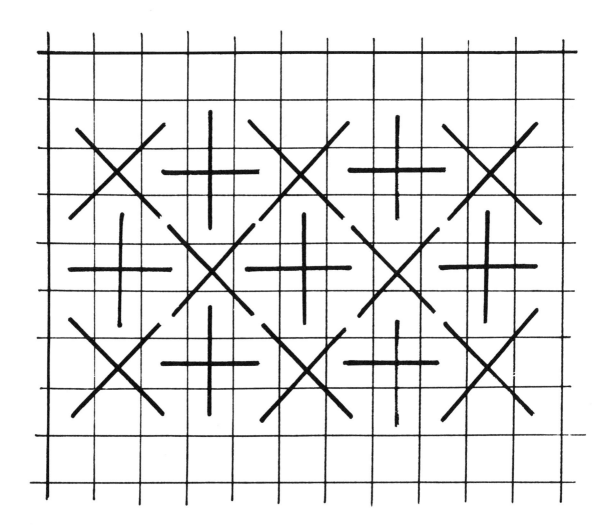

St. George and St. Andrew Stitches. This is a series of two stitches worked alternately. They are reversed on the second row. Must be done with the right amount of wool to cover the canvas without looking bulky.

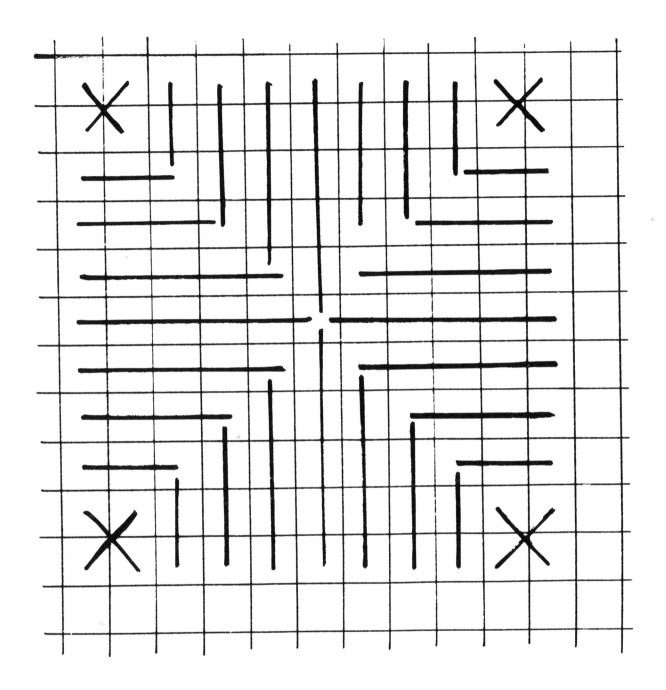

Triangle Stitch. This is a strongly patterned stitch which surprisingly enough makes a most effective background.

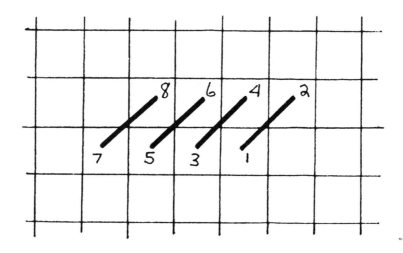

Tent Stitch. The best of all stitches for shading and fine detail. Worked from right to left. It is necessary to turn canvas around as you work on it.

Turkey Knot Stitch. Begin work on front of canvas. Work from bottom up.

Step 1. Needle down at A
up at B
down at C
up at A
Pull tightly

Step 2. Needle down at D
leave at loop
up at E
down at F
up at D
Pull tightly

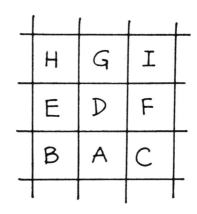

Step 3. Needle down at G
leave at loop
up at H
down at I
up at G
Pull tightly

Continue in this fashion. Loops may be left or may be cut for a "furry pile". Two strands work best.

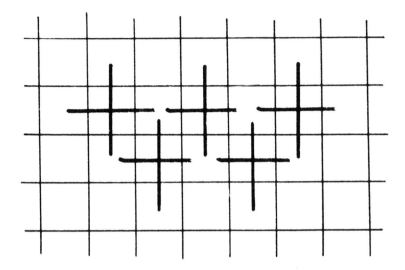

Upright Cross Stitch. It is used for backgrounds as well as detail work. Be sure all crosses cross in the same direction.

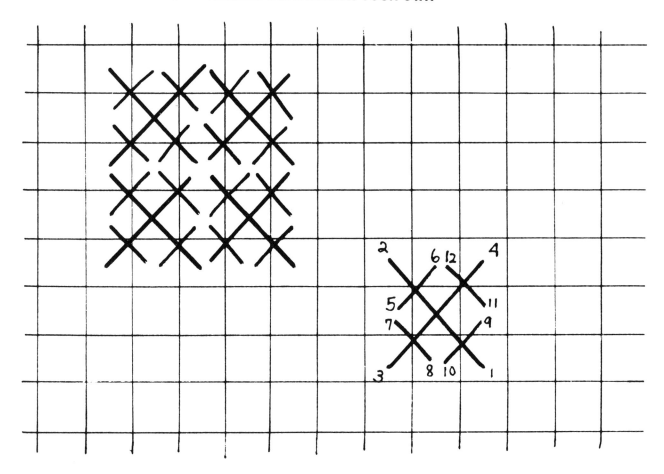

William and Mary Stitch. This is done with a large diagonal cross over 3 holes up and across with small diagonal stitches at right angles across the arms of the large cross. The large cross can be worked in wool, the small diagonal stitches in silk.

SUPPLIERS

The following shops will supply canvas by the yard and wool by
the ounce.

Needleloft
Mill Lane
Farmington, Connecticut   06032

Wizard Weavers
2701 Observatory Road
Cincinnati, Ohio   45208

Mariposa
39 Newbury Street
Boston, Massachusetts   02116

The Hook and I
21 Long Wharf Mall
Newport, Rhode Island   02840

Hanover Needlecraft
5 South Main Street
Hanover, New Hampshire   03755

Madeleine Horn Needlepoint
7 Parker Road
Osterville, Massachusetts   02655

Phalice's Thread Web
W. 1301 14th Avenue
Spokane, Washington   99204

The Needlecraft Shop
4501 Van Nuys Boulevard
Sherman Oaks, California   91403

Needlepoint à la Carte
325 South Woodward
Birmingham, Michigan   48011

Virginia Maxwell
3404 Kerby Drive
Houston, Texas   77006

Ann's Yarn House
505 West 24th Avenue
Pine Bluff, Arkansas   71601

The Wild Plum
517 Wilcox Street
Castle Rock, Colorado   80104

Natalie
144 North Larchmont Drive
Los Angeles, California   90004

Chapparal
2505 River Oaks Boulevard
Houston, Texas   77019

The Heirloom Shop
4330 North State Street
Jackson, Mississippi   39206

American Bequest Designs
36 Oak Street
Southington, Connecticut   06489

Needle Nook
6488 Central Avenue
St. Petersburg, Florida   33707

Evelyn Winter
5251 Ocean Boulevard
Sarasota, Florida   33581